How ~~to~~ Not to Make it in the Music Business

Memoir of a Singer/Songwriter

JIM BOWMAN

PUBLISHED BY FIDELI PUBLISHING, INC.

© Copyright 2018, Jim Bowman

All Rights Reserved.

No part of this book may be reproduced, stored in a retrieval system, or transmitted by any means, electronic, mechanical, photocopying, recording, or otherwise, without written permission from the author.

ISBN: 978-1-60414-999-9

For information, please contact
Fideli Publishing, Inc.:
info@fidelipublishing.com

www.FideliPublishing.com

*"I have heard of others out there
who try to wear my moniker.
Let there be no mistake.
I was, I am, and will always be
the original Camo Cowboy."*

~ Jim Bowman

Foreword

The first time I heard a Jim Bowman recording was when someone gave me a cassette tape that I played in my Bowhunting School in Pennsylvania. I hadn't had the pleasure of meeting Jim at that time.

I was at the Archery Trade Show in Nashville one night and he was on stage singing! I said to my wife Sheila, "that's him, that's the guy on the tape! That guy who does the poem that is called Hind Sight!" I still get tears in my eyes every time I hear that poem. When Jim finished singing, I walked to him, told him what a great job he did and let him know I had been playing his song at my bowhunting school for years! What a pleasure it was to finally meet him.

After that, Jim and I became good friends. We even went on a caribou hunt together. Jim continued to ask me questions about hunting and hunting camps all the while we were there. When he returned home from caribou hunting, he wrote a song for me and called it Wild

And Free! He totally hit the nail on the head with this song. He also wrote a song for the caribou camp that had everyone in tears.

Jim will tell you about not getting the Brass Ring, but I'm here to tell you he sure has helped a lot of folks get the Brass Ring in their lives, myself, included.

Bob Foulkrod
Hunting Legend

Author's Note

There's life the way you plan it. Then there is life the way it happens. Seldom are the two ever the same. When I was young I had grandiose dreams of being what the world calls a superstar. I just knew my name would be a household word. People would adore me and my mailbox would always be full of "music money" checks.

What transpired didn't come close to that, but I have had an amazing life full of twist and turns that to be honest, looking back, surprised even me.

The following pages highlight some of the more interesting times in my life.

Jim Bowman

Chapter One

I was singing at the Bluebird Café in Nashville, Tennessee, the night the movie *A Thing Called Love,* starring River Phoenix, premiered around the country. Because that movie was about songwriters, and the world-famous Bluebird Café, the place was packed. The only two empty seats in the house were at the table where my wife was sitting, watching the show. When two strangers came in and asked if they could sit down, she obliged.

When my set was over and I came back to the table, they both stood up and one of the guys extended his hand and said, "You are awesome! Jim, we're in town from LA to sign two artists—one male and one female—to a record deal. We think we just found our guy! Could you have lunch with us tomorrow to talk more?"

In my mind, I was thinking, *Finally*!

If you'd been in the passenger seat on my ride through life, you wouldn't believe that I could've done all the things I did, met all the people I was privileged to meet, and still not be a success in my chosen career. I'm sure I will only be able to touch the surface of all that's transpired through the years, but I think you'll enjoy helping me relive some of those memories of days gone by.

I was born to a poor Cumberland Mountain, Tennessee, family at a time when everyone was going north to the factories in Michigan, Indiana, and Ohio to literally keep from starving to death. My folks chose to escape to Dayton, Ohio. My Grandpa, who was a big influence in my life, lived there and stayed there until he died many years later.

My dad was one of those people who didn't know what he wanted to be when he grew up. He was never happy and was always changing jobs and dragging us, his family, from place to place. It was so bad that until I was in the sixth grade, I never went to the same school two years in a row. I'd just get to the point of making new friends, and then it would be time to go again.

When I was about six years old, we moved back to Tennessee for a short time. This time we were in Nashville, where my dad attended barber college. I can't remember too much about those days, but there are a few things that still stand out in my memory. This is when some of my best memories my Dad were created, because he was always doing stuff with me.

One day, he took me to the very top of the Life and Casualty building which was, in those days, the tallest building in Nashville. They called it "the air castle of the south." I remember the view of the city and the strange feeling I got — I just knew there was something for me somewhere in that town far below.

I remember my little sister, who was just a baby, getting Scarlett fever and how scared my mom and dad were. Her temperature got so high one night the doctor told my parents to put her in the bathtub and fill it with ice to bring her fever down.

The thing I remember most was the night my dad took me to the Ryman Auditorium, home of the Grand Ole Opry. I'm sure we saw a lot of acts that night, but the two I remember are Tex Ritter and Marty Robbins. I'm sure the reason I was taken with both of them was that they sang cowboy songs.

During our ride home, I remember my dad telling me about the first time he'd gone to the Opry when he was in the army. He said, "Son, that show tonight was pretty good, but you should've seen it when ol' Hank Williams was on the stage!" I still remember the reverence I heard in his voice as he talked about ol' Hank. I'd never heard him talk about anybody that way. I knew that somewhere down the road I wanted people to talk that way about me. I think that's when the music "bug" infected me.

As soon as Dad got out of barber school, we loaded up and headed back to Ohio. Then when I was nine years old, my folks finally decided we needed to be back in the mountains, and we moved back to Tennessee for the final time.

It was about that time that something else came into my life that would change it forever—a shiny new Sears and Roebuck arch-top guitar! I mowed lawns, sold Christmas cards and garden seeds, and did many odd jobs to buy that fine piece of musical sweetness. I also bought a Mel Bay chord book. Before long, I was strumming songs and I was off and running!

At that point, music had been quietly shaping me for years without me even knowing it. Growing up, I idolized singing cowboys like Gene Autry and Roy Rogers — especially ol' Roy. Little did I know that someday folks would come to hear me sing cowboy songs just the way my hero's had taught me as I sang along with their Saturday morning shoot 'em-ups.

The whole time we lived in exile in Ohio, my Mom would order records from the Jimmy Skinner radio show in Cincinnati. She was always playing Reno and Smily, MAC_Wiseman, Kitty Wells, and many other old-time artist. On Saturday nights, she'd listen to the Grand Ole

Opry on radio station WSM, and be treated to singers like Roy Acuff and Bill Monroe.

This was her way of keeping our family roots back in the Tennessee mountains. She accommmplished that and continuously bathed me in a constant shower of "high lonesome" music that somehow took root in my soul.

On weekends my dad and Uncle Kenneth would get together and play music in the backyard under the shade tree. My dad would be on mandolin and my uncle on guitar. I remember them being quite good. They had great harmony, but they never took it seriously.

At that time, we were living in Troy, Ohio. In the daytime, Uncle Kenneth worked at a factory called Tube Products with a couple of aspiring musicians by the name of Bobby and Sonny Osborn. He often talked

I was always going to be a singing cowboy. My Hop-a-Long Cassidy outfit.

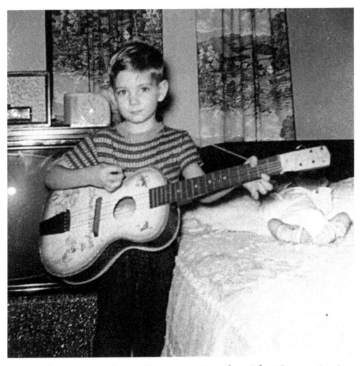

I was playing my Lone Ranger guitar but I bet I was singing "Happy Trails".

about how good their harmonies were as they sang while they worked. Years later, I would share the stage with them on a TV show in Nashville. It's a small world after all.

The first song I ever learned to play on my guitar was Johnny Cash's "Ghost Riders in the Sky". I also heard the local gospel groups every Sunday and sometimes at night time revivals in our little country church. I recognized that familiar "high lonesome" sound in the songs they were singing.

Somewhere, I found a copy of a Dotty Rambo songbook, and I started learning the songs of the greatest gospel songwriter of all time. To this day, I still love to hear Buck, Reba, and Dottie records as they sing songs like "One More Valley", "Come Spring" and "King Jesus".

The first time I remember standing up in front of people with my guitar to sing was on a Sunday morning at our church, the same church where I'd first walked the isle to accept Jesus. My little sister sang with me that morning.

I don't even remember what song we sang — I'm sure it was one of those Dottie Rambo songs — but I do remember the thrill I felt as the die of my life was cast. I soon formed my own gospel group, and for the next few years, we traveled from church to church, playing our own version of that "high lonesome" gospel.

If there is one thing in life I've learned, it's that Satan, that old adversary, is always pursuing your immortal soul. He was about to offer me my own apple from the garden of Eden.

Chapter Two

One day, I got a call from a pizza parlor owner from a nearby town. "Do you know any songs other than that church music?" he asked.

Now, every day of my senior year in high school I'd carried an old Yamaha guitar to school and I sang my heart out for my fellow classmates every chance I got. So I had quite a repretoire of songs from Neil Diamond to Merle Haggard to Glen Campbell, John Denver, and others. When I told him this, he said, "I have a college fraternity group coming in Saturday night. Would you like to play for them? I'll pay you a hundred dollars."

That was my first paying gig. Those college kids were downing beer by the pitcher, and the more they drank the better they liked my singing. This would be a great memory, except for what transpired later that night.

My pride and joy was my first car. It was a candy-apple-red, '69 fastback Mustang. On the way home from my debut as a "lounge lizard", I was feeling so good that I decided to let her out to run. There was a straight downhill stretch and I floored it. I was feeling the thrill and the *need for speed*, when something went wrong. All at once, I couldn't steer anymore — the steering wheel was loose in my hand. I had no control.

I later learned that a worn ball-joint had fallen off, leaving me a helpless passenger. I still remember the wreck like it was yesterday. I was traveling at a high rate of speed, yet everything seemed to slow down to slow motion like I was in a movie.

My car left the road and started riding a ditch line. My guitar, a big old sears amp, and a mic stand were in my back seat. When the car hit the ditch line, the amp hit me in the back of the head. I still remember the slow motion effect as the mic stand flew by my head and out through the windshield.

My car hit a culvert and became airborne. When it hit the ground, the front end was smashed against the ditch's dirt bank. Amazingly I was unhurt except for the knot on the back of my head. It was the wee hours of the morning, so there was no traffic, and in those days, no cell phones.

I got out and started walking toward town to find a wrecker. Thank goodness it wasn't long before a car came by and stopped to give me a ride. I learned later that my dad, who worked second shift, had seen my wrecked car and panicked as he searched for me at the wreck site.

Anyone with any sense might've seen that incident as an omen about a future in music, but then I've never been accused of having any sense.

♪ ♪ ♪

By the time I was out of high school, my mom and dad were on the road to divorce and I had to get away. My Mustang was good as new, so I pointed her north and headed back to Ohio to spend the summer with my Uncle Carlis and his family.

Carlis was my dad's youngest brother so he was closer to my age than my dad's. Our common bond was our love of horses. We went into a trading business together, buying, breaking, and selling horses.

One day, I found an ad in a local paper for a band looking for a singer. I answered it, and they hired me.

The band already had a job, so I was off to a running start for my singing career ... until the night the cops came in.

That night, when the band took a break, one of the officers came over and said, "You're a pretty good singer, boy. How old are you?"

Well it turned out you had to be 21 years old to be in an Ohio night club. When I confessed that I wasn't of age, the officers got on each side of me and escorted me to the parking lot. I'll never forget it. Freddy Hart was crooning

"Easy Loving", the biggest hit of the day, as Dayton's finest walked me out past the jukebox. That was the end of that gig.

♪ ♪ ♪

That old Sears and Roebuck guitar was not the only thing that had changed my life when I was nine years old. That same year, I carved my name into a beech tree on my grandpa's farm in Tennessee, along with the name of a little blonde-haired girl that rode on my school bus. Little did I know, she would later become my soul mate and life partner.

I sure missed her that summer while I was in Ohio. We wrote love letters to each other every day. It wasn't long before I felt the pull of the mountains again and headed my Mustang south, back toward home and the love of my life.

The die was cast by now and I couldn't escape it. I just couldn't see any future for me that didn't include music.

When I got back home, I put out a feeler so I could see if anyone was looking for a singing guitar player. I soon had gigs lined up at clubs and road houses all over the place.

If I could go back, I think I would've avoided that phase of my life. To a younger me, though, it was my college campus—a place to learn and pay my dues.

They say hindsight is twenty-twenty. I now know that to an ambitious young country singer, it became a pitfall journey that caused nothing but pain and bad memories for the people around me who knew and loved me. It led me down a path that was directly away from the one I was on the night I walked the aisle in that little country church.

Chapter Three

I had a couple of guys who were my wing-men in those days—my bass player and my drummer. They weren't just musicians, they believed in me and followed me through thick and thin. Honestly, looking back, they still are the closest thing I ever had to brothers.

At one time, there were three different people in the band, including me, who were named Jim. Every time someone said that name, we all answered. To help relieve the problem, Danny, my drummer, started calling me Bowjim. That name stuck and pretty soon that's what everyone was calling me.

When one club owner put out a newspaper ad advertising that we were going to be playing at his establishment, it said "This Friday and Saturday, Jim Bowman and the Bowgems!" That name stuck, too, and our band became the Bowgems.

When my son was born, I did an awful thing to him by making his middle name Bowgem. He must not have minded too much though, because when his son was born he gave him the same middle name.

One of the most satisfying things about being an entertainer is when you start getting fans who really like your music and think you have something special. Some of my early fans started a fan cub for me and, of course, it was called The Bowgem Fanclub. There were two chapters—one in Ohio, the other in Michigan.

One year they even had a booth at fanfare (now known as the CMA festival). They convinced me to wear a shirt they'd made for me that said, "Headed for Greatness". They were even able to get me to believe it. I was sure it was my destiny.

Fanfare 1973, "The Bowgem Fanclub".

♪ ♪ ♪

I started going to Nashville about that time in pursuit of my dreams. I was green as grass. I didn't know anybody in the music business, but I just knew that was where I belonged. I hit music row with a vengeance. I carried around a handful of tapes filled with songs I'd started writing, and I knocked on doors—lots of doors.

One of the first times I remember feeling like I was getting anywhere at all was the day I walked into the offices of the Wilborn Brothers. I knew that name because Teddy and Doyle had come into our living room via their TV show for as long as I could remember. What I didn't know was they had other brothers who ran their publishing company.

One of those brothers was the first person to show me the respect of sitting down to listen to my tape while I was still in the room. I pitched him a song called "Miss Music City, USA". When it was over, he smiled and said, "I like it, Jim. I know just who we'll pitch it to."

I was on top of the world as I left his office. I stopped at the door and turned around. I knew the music business sees many squirrelly people who think they have talent but really don't. They refer to them as squirrels. From the door I said, "I'm not a squirrel. I'm gonna make it in this business."

He almost busted a gut laughing, then said, "Jim, I knew you weren't a squirrel the minute you walked in here. We keep a bag of peanuts over in the corner. The squirrels always go straight for the nuts!"

I stopped by his office again about six months later, and my tape was still on his desk. I was relieved that he hadn't thrown it in the trashcan when I left. He even remembered my name. "Hey, Jim!" he said when I walked in. "Almost got you a cut. Loretta Lynn's little sister, Crystal Gail, was doing an album and we thought she was going to cut it, but at the last minute she went with another song." I later found out that that song was called "Don't it Make it my Brown Eyes Blue".

I recall another time when I walked into one of the hallowed offices of music row and was allowed to speak with one of the so-called moguls. When I walked into his office, he was smoking a cigar and was leaned back with his feet crossed upon his desk. He was a total cliché. When I gave him my tape, he walked over to his machine and put it in.

The whole time he was listening, he was staring at me with distain like I'd invaded his private sanctum and he needed to find a way to get rid of me fast. After listening, he asked, "Who told you you had any talent, boy? If you have a day job in whatever town you came from, you need to go back there and forget about a career in music."

With that, he tossed my tape into his wastebasket. I was shocked by his rudeness. My mamma would've skinned my hide if I ever treated anyone like that. I walked over, pulled my tape out of the trash and walked out of his office, slamming the door as I left. I was done for the day.

I'm not ashamed to say that I shed a good amount of tears during the two-hour drive home. When I got there, I walked into the house, gathered up every song I'd ever written — finished or not — and my Gibson guitar. I took everything outside and then slammed my guitar against the front porch, splintering it into a thousand pieces. After that, I gathered up all of the songs put them in a pile, and set them on fire.

I was done. I'd heard the truth from a professional, and now I knew I really didn't have any talent. I moped the rest of that week.

The next Monday, I went out and bought a new guitar. There are two things you should know about this story. The first is about the guitar I smashed. Years later, I walked into a vintage guitar store and saw the exact model Gibson as the one I'd sacrificed — its pricetag read $4,000! I still remember how stupid I felt at that moment.

Here is the vintage Gibson that I demolished after a day on Music Row.

The second is the music mogul. Years later, I showcased at the world famous Stock Yards Lounge. When my show was over, a familiar-looking man met me at the edge of the stage with his hand extended. "You"re great!" he gushed. "Why haven't I ever heard about you?"

"You have," I said, without shaking his hand. "You caused me to do some things I still regret after a song-pitching session in your office down on the Row." Then, I just turned and walked away, leaving him standing there with his hand extended. Many times I've laid awake at night wondering if that evening I might have turned my back on my one big chance at stardom.

Chronological order is something I am having trouble with as I try to unpack all of these old memories. I think the reason is because so much was happening in my life on different levels at this time, and I was also living in two worlds — the real one and the one I imagined for myself in music.

In the real world, I'd married that little blonde-haired girl I talked about earlier, and together we'd brought another beautiful little blonde-haired girl into the world. She was the center of our universe.

Now, I was a husband and a daddy, even though I was still just a kid myself. With this new responsibility, my thinking and plan of action had to change. I decided to go to broadcasting school to become a radio disc jockey. I thought this would at least keep me close to music while providing an income for my new family.

Almost at the same time, I also became an employee of Opryland, USA. I wasn't working as a performer. I was doing every menial task needed by the park. So, I was working and going to school, burning the candle at both ends. Both of those endeavors hold a treasure trove full of memories that should be revisited.

First, the school. Elkins Institute of Broadcasting was one of two businesses in a building on Eighth Avenue in Nashville. There was a bar downstairs and the school was upstairs. *Show me an Ivy League school with that perk!*

I have many memories of that time, but I don't think anything stands out quite like the night of the shooting. We were playing disc jockey, spinning records and reading scripts and news, just like we were really on the air. Suddenly we heard what sounded like a huge explosion downstairs. Plaster even fell off the walls and ceiling. The instructors wouldn't let us go see what had happened, but one of them went to check it out.

When he came back, he reported that someone had walked in off the street and shot the bar's piano player with a shotgun. That night after class, I went to my van to get ready to go home and found that someone had broken out a window and stolen my shotgun and deer rifle that had been hanging on my gun rack. I've often wondered if that piano player was shot with my shotgun. I made a police report that night but the guns were never recovered.

Another great story concerns the night I graduated. There was no ceremony or anything. When the school thought you were ready to pass the FCC exam, they shipped you out.

One night, my instructor informed me that I was ready, and said if I could make it to Atlanta the following morning by 9 a.m. I could take the test for my first-class FCC license. He told me one of the other students was ready too, and suggested we might want to carpool.

Well, it turned out the other guy was African-American. We talked it over, tossed a coin, and it was decided that he would drive. We argued over the music on the radio all the way down there. He wanted Motown, while I preferred country. It was his car and his radio, so I got schooled on soul!

I came face to face with racial discrimination that night when we stopped at a little store in Georgia to get a cold drink and use the rest room. I was standing in front of the drink cooler, when three good ol' boys came over and asked me, "What you doing traveling with that nigger? He your boyfriend or something?"

My first impulse was to smash somebody's face, but then I realized I was a long way from home and outnumbered. So, I just told them the situation. They weren't too sympathetic and said, "Well you need to get on out of here and don't be caught around here anymore with that black SOB."

I was glad when we got back on the road. I didn't even argue about the music the rest of the way there.

As part of our school deal, we had a room reserved close to the place where we'd be taking our test in a few hours. After we checked in, I went straight to bed. After a full day at Opryland and school and then the time on the road, I was bushed. As I was fading off to sleep, I thought I heard a door open and close.

It seemed like I'd just got to sleep when someone was shaking me. I opened one eye, and there was my fellow traveling companion with a lady of the night on each arm. "Wake up, brother," he said. "I done gone out and found us two ladies to help us celebrate our new careers … one for you and one for me!"

I turned over and went back to sleep. I don't know what he did the rest of the night, but when we took our test the next morning, I passed and he failed. It was a long, quiet trip back to Nashville.

Chapter Four

Opryland USA was a magical place. My first job there was cleaning the bathrooms. I didn't do that for long, as I advanced quickly up the ladder. Eventually, I became radio dispatcher for the entire park.

I met a lot of celebrities during my tenure there, and I started collecting memorabilia from all the stars. I had things like personalized guitar picks from artists like Buck Owens, Tom T. Hall and Merle Haggard. Charlie McCoy gave me one of his harmonicas, and Archie Campbell gave me one those huge ol' stogie cigars he always smoked on the set of *Hee Haw*.

I think one of my favorite treasures came from the original King of Country Music, Roy Acuff. I had met Mr. Acuff several times out in the park and talked with him briefly about some of the things in my collection.

One day, I was working when this announcement came over the park intercom: *"Jim Bowman, please report to the employees cafeteria."* I couldn't imagine what I'd done! When I reported to the cafeteris, they directed me to a table far in the back and said someone was waiting for me there.

When I arrived, there sat Bashful Brother Oswald, Charlie Collins, and Mr. Acuff, who said, "Sit down, son. I want to buy your lunch."

I can't describe how I felt at that moment. Remember how I told you about how my momma would listen to the Grand Ole Opry when we lived in Ohio? Well, I was having lunch with a group of fellows we'd listened to so many times — and they were buying lunch!

The best part came when Mr. Acuff reached into his pocket and pulled out one of his trademark yo-yos. He said, "I was thinking about your collection the other day, and I thought you might like to have one of these. Did you know I gave one of these to Richard Nixon when he visited the Opry?" That yo-yo is still one of my most treasured possessions.

One morning, many years later, I got up and turned on the news only to hear that Roy Acuff, the King of Country Music, had passed away. Within an hour, I had written a song for Mr. Acuff that I still hope to sing on the stage of the Grand Ole Opry someday. And yes, I will spin that yo-yo.

Another person I met worked with me there in the park. His name was Deford Bailey, Jr. His father was an old-school Grand Ole Opry legend from the early days of George D. Haye, the solemn old judge. Deford Baily is known as the first black man to be a member of the Opry cast. He played harmonica and is remembered for his song "Fox Chase".

One night, I was taking my break the same way I usually did. I had sneaked back to where the park instruments were stored and was entertaining myself by singing and playing one of their Martin guitars. I thought I was all alone, so I was lettin' 'er rip, when this black guy came gliding around the corner. He looked at me for a moment, like he couldn't believe his eyes. "Boy, you sure are a good singer," he said. "I thought the radio was playin' back here, and I was gonna turn it off!"

In the conversation that followed, the subject of the yo-yo Mr. Acuff had given me came up. Within two days, I was in possession of a blues harp that had been used by legendary harmonica player Deford Baily on the stage of the Grand Ole Opry. The best part is, I never even asked for it — Junior just wanted me to have it as a gift. What a gift! What a treasure!

About this same time, I heard about auditions for a new TV show that WSM-TV was planning to produce called *Young Country*.

Now WSM is a legendary powerhouse media company based in Nashville, Tennessee. Their claim to fame is The Grand Ol Opry, *a country music show that has run for decades on the country radio airwaves. They also have a TV station in Nashville.*

The auditions were going to be held at different times and places around the country. When I started checking my busy school/work schedule, the only one I could possibly make was the one in McMinnville, Tennessee, because it was late in the evening.

I don't even remember why, but I almost missed it and came in late for the audition. I was the last person they were going to audition for the show ever, anywhere. I remember I was flustered because of almost missing the audition, so I thought I'd better sing something I knew I wouldnt forget the words to. I chose Merle Haggard's "Hungry Eyes" and Kris Kristofferson's "Me and Bobby McGee".

"Why haven't I heard of you?" the producer asked me after I finished.

I drove away that night, happy to be a cast member of a real TV show. Other members of the cast included a band of cousins who would come to be known as The

Kentucky Headhunters, but at that time were known as The Itchy Brothers.

Also in the cast were Billy Troy, the son of Flatt and Scruggs dobro player, Josh Graves; and Blake Williams, a banjo player who later became one of Bill Monroe's Bluegrass Boys. There were a lot of others who were all very talented. I'm proud I was chosen to be part of that alumni.

I was out of school and ready to get on with my life. The morning I told my boss I was leaving Opryland USA, he wasn't happy with my decision. He said, "Jim, we've been watching you and think you could have a great career right here at Opryland. Let's think about this. As you know, the Opry House will be finished soon. With your FCC license, we could probably put you in charge of sound and lighting for the Opry. If you don't want to do that, there's always the Opryland Hotel. You're a smart guy, so I know we can find you a good position over there. We sure don't want to lose you. So think about it."

I was young and stupid. I'd gone to broadcasting school and was determined to be on the radio. I left Opryland USA and went to work at WBRY, an AM/daytime-only station that sat squarely in the middle of a cemetery in Woodbury, Tennessee. *Yep, I was making all the right career decisions on my way to the top!*

I was still playing clubs every weekend with my band during this time. Many of them were places I wouldn't be caught dead in and I wouldn't have been there if they weren't paying us to play. I don't talk too much about those places because they're not uplifting memories. Still, I'll share a couple of those stories for the entertainment value that you might find in them.

We were living in a doublewide mobile home at the time of this incident. That morning, my wife, who was an RN, had just finished a hard week of hospital shifts, and I'd played at a club until the wee hours of the morning. It was a Saturday, and we were sleeping in, trying to get caught up on some rest. Suddenly, someone was knocking loudly on our front door. When I opened it, I found the local Sheriff waiting. "Jim," he said, "I need you to take a ride with me."

I put on some clothes and got into his car. I had no clue what was going on. Then, he picked up his radio and said, "Suspect in custody."

"WHOA!" I said. "Suspect in what?"

"Do you know a man by the name of __?" he asked.

"Yeah, our band played in his club a couple months back," I said.

"Well, he was murdered last night. Your business card was in his cash register and the Tennessee Bureau of Investigation wants to talk to you."

When we got to the sheriff's office, the TBI agents were waiting for us. They wasted no time getting to my interrogation. They sat me in a chair, and first one would ask me a whole list of questions, and then the other would ask the same questions again but a different way. They did this over and over. I guess they were trying to catch me in a lie.

After a while, they decided I must be innocent and told me I could go. I found out later that the murdered man had been killed by his son.

♪ ♪ ♪

Talk to any old club musician for any length of time, and the subject of bar fights is bound to come up. They just come with the territory. There's usually nothing funny about most of them, but every once in a while one will make you laugh.

Very early in my career as a club singer, one of these funny times occurred. My usual drummer had told us he had to have a few weeks off to spend time with his family, so I hired a temp to take his place.

On the night this fight occurred, the new drummer had brought his girlfriend to the club with him. When our guitar player's brother showed up, we found out the drummer's girlfriend was his ex-girlfriend.

Throughout the night, the guitar player's brother would come up to the stage to talk to his brother, and they would get just loud enough that we could hear them but couldn't make out what they were saying. Each time, I could see the brother glaring at the drummer.

Stay with me now.

When we took our third break of the night, I saw my guitar player go back and almost drag his brother to the front door. I figured they were going out to talk things over. But when the guitar player didn't show up after the break, I went out to look for him.

When I got to the parking lot, there they were, rolling around on the ground, throwing punches. Both of them were dirty and had blood on their faces. I quickly broke them up — we still had another set to play. The brother went on to his car and left.

On the way back into the building, I asked the guitar player what was going on. To this day, I still laugh when I think about his answer. "My brother was going to jump on that new drummer you hired because of that girl," he said. "I had to bring him out here and explain to him just how hard a good drummer is to find!"

We were hired into a new club to play for two weeks and told that we would be paid at the end of that time. Two weeks passed, and no one offered to pay us. I went by the club several times to talk to the owners, but apparently they were slipping out the back door every time they saw me coming.

Eventually, I guess the girl tending bar either felt sorry for me or got tired of seeing me stop by. Anyway, she said, "Look, I really enjoyed your music, and you seem like nice guys, so I'm just going to tell you. You're not going to get paid. They've done this to two other bands. After they got fed up with not getting paid and quit showing up, they just hired another band." I asked her if she was sure about this, and she said she was.

It was the middle of the afternoon, so there were hardly any customers in the place. I walked out to my van, and when I came back I was carrying a little short twenty-guage, called a Hooda that I kept in the van for protection. I walked over to the jukebox and fired both barrels into the speaker area. As I walked out, I said, "Tell those two thieves to use the money they owe me to fix their jukebox."

You have to understand those were different times. Anyway, I started telling every band I knew not to play for those guys. Their club didn't last long without live entertainment.

One of the clubs I played regularly was a watering hole for oil people. There was a surge in drilling in Tennessee and Kentucky, and money was flowing right along with the oil. It was nothing for someone to stick a hundred dollar bill into my pocket when they asked for their favorite song.

Those were wild and crazy days and nights. I made a lot of friends, and we found ourselves playing at private events for the oil people back in their hometowns. I could share a lot of stories about all that went on, but this is the one that fits the theme of our narrative best.

One of the oil men invited me to bring my band up to a marina in Kentucky and play for a houseboat party. When we arrived, we set up on the dock where houseboats were anchored as far as we could see on both sides of the dock.

We had just started playing when people began handing us margaritas in huge glasses. We already knew the oil people knew how to party, and now we knew this was going to be a par-tay!

After we'd played our second set and announced we were going to take a break, my friend who hired us invited me down to take a look at his new houseboat. He said he had something he wanted to talk to me about.

There were a lot of beautiful boats anchored on each side as we walked down the dock. As we neared the end, he pointed out his boat, anchored crossways at the end. It was bigger than any two boats there. I mean it was *huge!*

We went aboard, and I was getting the tour when all at once he turned and said, "As you can see, Jim, I've finally made it. Monday morning, my company will go on the New York Stock Exchange and start selling shares. At breakfast at my home this morning, we had a family meeting. My wife and kids have everything we've ever wanted, and now we want to help someone else — give them a leg up. We put it to a vote, and it was unanimous. We chose you."

With that, he reached into his shirt pocket and handed me a check. I just about fainted when I saw the figure written on it. There were more zeros than I'd ever seen! *Here was my chance to make a record in Nashville!*

My dream could've come true, but what did I do? I said, "Look, we're drinking right now, but if you really want to invest this in my career, let's get together later with some attorneys, draw up some contracts, and I'll try to be a good investment for you."

With that, I tore up the check and handed it back to him. Within a month, the bottom fell out of the oil business, and my friend, along with many others, found himself bankrupt.

Chapter Five

One of the radio stations I worked at early on was in Cookeville, Tennessee, and was owned by an elderly lady. I was just getting settled in to the early morning shift. I'd learned to turn on the transmitter and fill out the logs and do weather and news without too many mistakes.

One morning, she called me into her office. When she asked me to come in and close the door, I felt like a kid who'd been sent to the principle's office. The program director was already in there, sitting in a chair in the corner. When I saw his face, I knew I was not going to like what was about to take place.

"Mr. Bowman," she said, "I have just learned that you play in a band." Then she just sat there looking at me, waiting for me to respond.

"Yes, ma'am, I do," I replied.

"I'm sorry, but I'm going to have to let you go."

"Why? Because I am a musician? This is a radio station. You make your money off musicians!" I replied.

"It's my company policy," she said. "Sooner or later, you're going to have a gig booked at a time when you're scheduled to work, so I'm just going to have to let you go now."

"Why don't you wait until something like that happens?" I asked.

"No, my mind's made up. You are dismissed, effective immediately."

Just like that I was fired, not because of anything I did, but because of what my boss thought I might do. In today's world, that would be grounds for a lawsuit. Back then I was just unemployed.

♪ ♪ ♪

The *Young Country* show that I had done on WSM introduced me to a few people, and soon I was booked onto the *Ralph Emery Early Morning Show* also on WSM in Nashville. Soon, I was a semi-regular along with a small group of young singers, including Lori Morgan, Tom Grant and Donna Meade, who later became Mrs Jimmy Dean.

It was on that show that I began to polish myself. I had an audience who was seeing me for the first time on a regular basis. I was starting to get some much needed publicity.

One morning, I learned a valuable show business lesson. Ralph always introduced me as being from Celina, a town down the road from where I really lived. That morning, he'd already introduced me, and my microphone was hot when he said, "Wait, I have a note here from a lady over there in Celina, Jim, who says she really enjoys hearing you sing. She said to be sure and read this on an odd morning. What do you think she meant by that?"

I was on the spot and grabbed for an ad-lib. "Maybe she means on a morning when you show up for work and don't have a guest host," I replied. I could tell by the look on his face that this seasoned media professional did not like what had just come out of my mouth on live TV.

"You doing standup comedy in your act now?" he asked. "Why don't you leave that to me and just sing us a song?"

I did, but I was never booked onto the *Ralph Emery Show* again. Another valuable lesson learned.

I was pounding the streets of Music Row every chance I got, with little success. I found a new classroom at Tootsie's Orchard Lounge on lower Broadway. Like a fly on the wall, I was privileged to be in there at times when people like Waylon Jennings, Willie Nelson and Roger Miller were there, just drinking and telling music business stories— learning about the business I was trying to break into. I was like a sponge, soaking up every word that came out of their famous mouths.

During this time, I became friends with the proprietor, Tootsie Bess. Tootsie was like everybody's mother. When she found I was chasing the music dream, I became one of her children. When I made my first 45 record, she put it on her jukebox just like I was a somebody famous.

Lone Star beer was a big fad in those days. One afternoon, she took out a felt tip marker and wrote on my beer can: "To Jim, from Tootsie". That Lone Star can still holds a valuable place in my collection of memorabilia.

After I made that first record, I was booked onto the *Earnest Tubb Record Shop* radio show. It was on late nights on WSM right after the Grand Ole Opry. Guests on the Saturday night show, got their records played all day on the speaker outside of the store on lower Broadway so all the tourist could hear who was going to be on that night.

The afternoon of the day I was to be on, I stopped by to tell Tootsie I was going to be singing. She went over to the jukebox, put in a bunch of quarters and punched up my record to play. I can't describe the feeling I got when I walked out of Tootsie's bar on lower Broadway and could hear myself singing from the speakers at the

Record Shop. "Yep," I told myself. "I'm gonna own this town."

That night, I was introduced by Little Jimmy Dickens, who gave me one of the best introductions I've ever received. I was accompanied by Conway Twitty's band as I sang a song I'd written for my wife. I was sure my feet were firmly set on the path to stardom.

Speaking of Conway Twitty, when I was on the *Young Country* show, I was asked, along with a female cast member, to open a show for Conway in Bowling Green, Kentucky. The show was outdoors in an amphitheater, and Conway had packed it. I could feel the electricity in the air from the very start. The crowd was rowdy, and singing for them was fun.

When I finished, I was leaving the stage as Conway was walking out. As I got to the wings, I heard him say, "Hello, Darlin.'" The response was deafening. The crowd was already on their feet, but I noticed something. It was mostly women. The ladies had given Conway Twitty a standing ovation after just two words ... "Hello Darlin'"!

Chapter Six

I've never liked contests, talent or writing, but when you're trying to get noticed in show business, sometimes they're a necessary evil.

The radio station where I was working at the time was promoting one of the nationwide Country Showdowns that guaranteed a recording contract among a bunch of other lucrative prizes, so I entered—just me and my guitar. I won the local challenge and then the regional. Then I was off to the nationals in West Tennessee.

I was amazed by the quality of talent I heard warming up at the nationals. It was mostly bands from all over the country, and for the first time, I felt that I was in over my head. I worried that I really didn't belong there. But I had come that far, so when it was time to perform, I walked out to the microphone and sang my song.

Afterward, I went up into the cheap seats to watch the rest of the show. In a little while, this guy came up, sat down, and introduced himself to me. He said he was one of the disc jockeys hosting this show. I was about to learn another valuable show business lesson.

He said, "Jim, you were really good out there, and if things were the way they should be, you'd win this thing. I hate to tell you this, but it was fixed from the get-go. There are a couple of girls who will perform here in a little bit. They call themselves Sweethearts of the Rodeo. They sing at Loretta Lynn's Dude Ranch, and this whole thing was staged to launch their careers. (One of the girls is married to Vince Gill.)

Sure enough, at the end of the day, Sweethearts of the Rodeo won that recording contract, and as they say, "The rest is history."

♪ ♪ ♪

I always remember this story when Saint Patrick's Day rolls around, because that's when it happened. I'd agreed to do some shows with Sherry and Sheila Aldrich from the *Lawerence Welk Show*. They were from Knoxville, so I guess that's how we crossed paths; I really don't remember. They hired me and my band to play at some nursing homes with them over in the Smoky Mountains.

We played one evening for a group in Gatlinburg, and the next morning we were supposed to play at another place in North Carolina. I was traveling in a van in those days, so after the show we loaded up the equipment,

Sherry and Sheila, one of their cousins, and the band and headed over the mountains.

At Blowing Rock, North Carolina, we had to stop. We needed to stretch, and the girls had been asking for a restroom break for miles. We saw a "Free Green Beer" sign and pulled in.

After a few toasts to Saint Paddy, we knew we needed to get back on the road. The Aldridge girls said their grandpa lived on Grandfather Mountain, so we were going to rest there until time for the show. We all climbed into the back of the van with the equipment and laid down on the floor to try to get some rest. It had been a long day and night, and it was getting late.

My drummer and friend, Danny Scott, volunteered to drive. I've thought many times about what happened that night, and I've come to realize that it was a God thing. I still remember how relaxed I felt and how well I was sleeping.

Suddenly, I came wide awake, sat up, and looked out through the windshield. All I could see were stars. No trees, no road signs, no houses—just stars. We might as well have been flying in a 747. When I glanced at Danny, I noticed his head was laid over to one side, and I knew he was asleep. The driver was asleep! I yelled as loud as I could, "DANNY!"

He sat up and hit the brakes, all at the same time. When the van came to a stop, I got out to look things over. The front wheels were about a foot from the edge of Grandfather Mountain. If you've ever been there, you know that a fall there is a long way down. I wouldn't be here to write this account if we'd gone over. God was not through with someone in that van!

I tried to keep our band busy, booking different venues here and there. We all needed the money, so we took a lot of jobs we didn't really want to do. One of these, I'd just as soon forget.

We were booked into the lounge of a major motel chain that sat on the side of an Interstate highway for the weekend. We came in early on Friday afternoon and set up our equipment, then left to grab a bite to eat. We came back in time to play.

From the very first note of the first song, something just didn't seem right. First of all, we were used to seeing lady bartenders everywhere we played. Not here—they were all guys. Then the clientele started to arrive, two by two, and all the guys in the band started looking nervous.

It hit us all at the same time. We were all young and naïve, but we realized we were performing in a gay bar! "Shut 'er down boys!" I said. "We're out of here!"

We started loading up our equipment and the lounge manager came out, mad as fire. "You can't do this!" he shouted "I'll sue you!"

"Sue away," I said. "We have our standards, and this sure ain't it." We were all in shock as we pulled out of the parking lot, but a couple of miles down the road, we just started laughing ...

I was working through the week at WSMT in Sparta, Tennessee. I'd worked my way up to program director by this time and on weekends, I was playing clubs with my band.

One day, the boss came in and told me we were going to host a talent show at a mall in McMinnville, Tennessee. It was for a new show country star Bill Anderson was producing, called *You Can Be A Star*. They wanted me to MC the contest and to bring my band to play during dead times between acts. The winner would get to appear on the new TV show and get a chance to win a recording contract.

It was a great experience, and I couldn't believe the number of acts that performed that day. Toward the end of the afternoon, I told the crowd there would be a short break while the judges compared notes and chose a winner. Along with a couple of judges and the producer of the TV show, we went off to a little office the mall had provided.

We had no more than sat down when the producer said, "Jim, I've only seen one person today that I'd like to have on the show, and that's you. If you'll sign a contract with us for five years, giving us exclusive rights to you and letting us publish any songs you write, you'll be the first season's winner of *You Can Be a Star*."

This immediately hit me the wrong way. I didn't like it when that was done to me at the Country Showdown, and I didn't want to be the one to do it to all the people I'd just watched singing their hearts out to try to be a winner. Besides, five years seemed like an eternity, so I declined. *Once again, I made a brilliant career move that was bound to take me to the top.*

♪ ♪ ♪

I worked for several years at a radio station WDEB in Jamestown, Tennessee. I lived in Livingston the whole time, so I had a commute that took me about an hour each way through some beautiful but truly wild and scenic landscape. I spent many of those drives in meditation about my future and all I planned to do.

One afternoon, when I arrived at the station, the boss took me into his office and gave me some special operating instructions. It seems a young man had shot his own father that day and was incarcerated in the Fentress County Jail.

Because the station had chosen to run a news story about it, death threats had been being phoned in all day. He told me not to answer the phone, to lock both the front door and the control room door, and not to stop for anyone on my drive home that night. My shift was quite uneventful, though I was nervous the whole time.

Coming out of Jamestown going toward my home was a pretty good drop in altitude as I came off the Cumberland Plataue, down the mountain. Toward the bottom of that drop is Indian Creek Bridge, which spans a river. In those days, I drove an old Ford Econoline van that I'd remodeled with walls and shag carpet to haul my band equipment on weekends.

It was a really dark night, and I wasn't thinking about anything in particular as I approached that bridge. Suddenly, I saw two flashes of light just as I heard the reports of a shotgun. The next thing I heard was a sizzling sound, like bacon frying in a pan. My windshield fell completely out onto the highway just as two car headlights came on and momentarily blinded me. Then, a little red car came rushing straight at me. As they drove past me, headed back up the mountain, I could make out two men in the car, but I couldn't see their faces.

I instantly got mad. I made a u-turn and took off wide-open after my attackers. Suddenly, it hit me. *You idiot! Those men just shot at you! You have no weapon, and you're chasing them?* That's when common sense kicked in, and I decided to turn around and just go home.

From that night on, I never went anywhere without carrying some sort of protection.

♪ ♪ ♪

It was while I was working at the radio station in Jamestown that something good finally happed to my career. The fellows who owned our station also owned a car dealership, and occasionally they would have my band play at promotions they did.

At one of those promotions, we shared the stage with another band from East Tennessee called the Kountry Kings. Since I didn't have East Tennessee TV, I'd never heard of them, but they were really good. I later found out that many of them had been road musicians for some big country acts like Don Gibson and Red Sovine. We all played our songs, the bosses sold some cars, and we all went home.

A few days later, I received a call from one of the The Kountry Kings band members. He told me his name and that he was the steel player/band leader for the group. "Really enjoyed your singing the other day," he said, "and that's why I'm calling. We're losing our lead singer soon, and we wondered if you'd like to take his place."

He went on to tell me that they had a weekly TV show in Knoxville, sponsored by Clayton Mobile Homes. They played somewhere every weekend, and they had a contract with radio station WIVK to be the opening act for all of their Country Shindig Promotions at Municipal Coliseum.

By the end of that phone conversation, a new chapter of my life was about to begin. I was going to be a Kountry King!

Chapter Seven

I continued to work as a disc jockey. That was my bread and butter. Two nights a week, I would drive to Knoxville to film the TV show. Every weekend, we played a gig somewhere, and they were all interesting.

Stoney, our band leader, told us one day that we'd been booked to play for the prisoners at a prison called Brushy Mountain. I'll never forget that experience. I think of it every time I hear Johnny Cash sing "Folsom Prison Blues".

First of all was the location. The prison was in Petros, Tennessee—a desolate mountain area surrounded on three sides by huge mountains. The only way in or out was through the front gates. Any escapee would be easily caught by dogs before he could make it over the mountains.

At the first check point, our vehicles, equipment, and our persons were searched. Nothing that was not supposed to be there was getting into this prison. Then, we were given instructions to stay on the stage and not to talk to any of the prisoners. They told us something was up with the inmates, but they weren't sure what it was. They said to just do our show, follow protocol, and then everything would be all right. After that, we were escorted into the main prison area.

I'll never forget the sound of that gate locking behind us. I can't imagine how it would be to know that you were there to stay.

Our show went great. We'd brought a girl singer with us, and those inmates loved her. She was the first woman many of them had seen in a long, long time.

The crowd was so receptive that we soon forgot where we were and just got into the show. When it was over, people came to the stage just like any other show, asking for autographs. I'd forgotten about our briefing and jumped down off the stage to sign some autographs.

I was signing for one guy, making small talk, when I asked him what he was in for. Without hesitation he said, "I killed three members of my family." I realized I wasn't in Kansas anymore and quickly found my way back onto the stage.

We later learned that James Earl Ray, who had allegedly killed Martin Luther King Jr., was in our audience that day. The "something" the prison had not been sure about was the planning of his escape. Two weeks after we entertained him, he went over the wall.

Chapter Eight

Jake Butcher was a wealthy Tennessee banker who made a run for Governor. We were hired to play at a fundraiser at his home one night — the dinners that evening were $1,000 a plate. His home was beautiful, and the Who's Who of East Tennessce aristocrats were there.

We'd played a couple of sets for the folks to dance to, then Con Hunley arrived. Con was a Knoxville singer who could croon with the best of them. He was soon seated at the piano with an adoring crowd gathered around him. He was their favorite son, and he knew how to milk it. I heard someone say, "Look at that. He's singing to a state Supreme Court Judge, a neurosurgeon, several lawyers, doctors and bankers, and they all adore him."

Jake Butcher was never elected as Tennessee's Governor. As for Con Hunley, I worked many shows with him and even filled in for him at his regular gig in Knoxville when he started to become popular and went on the road.

♪ ♪ ♪

The Kings were booked at the Tennessee Agricultural and Industrial Fair for two weeks with the Oak Ridge Boys. I was so excited! When I'd been singing Gospel music, their song "Jesus is Coming Soon" was one of my favorites.

They had only recently switched over to the Country Music field, and now they were playing on my home court. I came in early one day and decided I would gather up my courage and go by their dressing room and say hi.

I knocked on the door, and a voice said, "Come on in." There sat one of the "Mighty Oaks" with several lines of cocaine laid out on the table in front of him. I quickly left, having learned that people are not always who you think they are.

Not long after that, he left the group for a while and was replaced by another singer. Sometimes you just can't unsee things you've seen.

♪ ♪ ♪

The Kountry Kings had a contract with WIVK, a huge country station in Knoxville, to be the opening act and house band for all of the concerts they promoted. They called the concerts 'Country Shindigs." If I weren't already addicted to show business, the "Country Shindigs" would have done it. The stage of Municipal Colosseum was the first place I ever felt the glow of spotlights shining on me as I performed for thousands of excited concert-goers. With our TV show, we were local celebrities, but we were opening for the giants of the music industry.

Over a period of two years, I was privileged to share the stage with practically every artist that was being heard on American radio at the time. We did shows with people like Kenny Rogers, Reba McEntire, the Statler Brothers, the Oak Ridge Boys, the Gatlins, Eddie Rabbit, and the list went on and on.

Charlie Pride was on one of the shows. A few days after that show, I recieved a call from Alex Harvey, a ventriloquist who worked with Charlie's show. He said, "Charlie Pride's piano player and front man, Ronnie Milsap, is about to go out on his own, and Charlie wanted me to call you. He really liked your singing, and if you can play piano, he wants to hire you to take Milsap's place."

"Sorry," I said, "I don't play piano but you should call our piano player. He's also a good singer."

Long story short, Danny Hutchins got the job, and to this day, still plays piano for Country Charlie Pride.

I had been given the opportunity to be a positive influence on someone else's life. They say all good things come to an end, and after a few years, the members of the band started to have different interests, and we just drifted apart. The Kountry Kings became a memory.

WIVK Country Shindig with the Kendalls and my friend and guitar player Ken Bonham at far left.

Kountry Kings with Charlie McClain.

Chapter Nine

I got a call from a club owner I had played for in the past, who wanted me to do a songwriters' night with some of his Nashville friends. I did so, and quickly made friends with the other writers who were on the show.

Wayne Carson had written some monster hits. "The Letter" was a rock and roll hit that had made him some money. He was also a co-writer of Willie Nelson's "Always on my Mind". There was also Ronny Reno, son of Bluegrass legend Don Reno, who had worked with people like Johnny Cash and Merle Haggard.

I started hanging around my new friends at Carson's Nashville apartment. It was another "college course" in my music business education.

Wayne was a great song writer, but as I spent time with him I started to realize his lyrics came from a tortured soul. He'd lost in love and found refuge for his broken heart in pills and tequila. He dealt with heartbreak by writing his feelings down to music, and the world loved the lyrics.

I met a lot of people in that little apartment just off music row. One night, we were trying to write a song when there was a knock at the door. It was Tony Joe White of Poke Sallet Annie fame. He had just stopped by to say hello.

Another time, Carl Perkins showed up. He was doing a show in Nashville, and the airlines had lost his guitar. Wayne loaned him one of his.

We were always having "guitar pulls" where everyone would take a turn singing the latest lyric they had come up with. It was at one of these events that I met Cal Miller. Cal was Carson's neighbor across the hall. He was attending the little "guitar pull" and we were listening to someone's latest and greatest inspiration while drinking the mandatory beers.

"I really want to be a songwriter, he told me, but I can't find anyone who will write with me," Cal said.

Now, my creative juices were flowing, and I'd had just enough to drink to make me brave enough to jump in. In those days, I'd write at the drop of a hat, and sometimes I threw down my own hat! "I'll write with you," I said. "If we had a quiet place, we could write something right now!"

He said, "I live right across the hall, and I have a guitar over there."

So we excused ourselves and headed on over to his apartment to write. "Got any ideas?" I asked as I sat down.

He never even hesitated with his answer. "I've been thinking that a song about a cowboy's idea of the perfect woman. That would be a good song."

That's all it took. Within thirty minutes, we were back at the "guitar pull" and I was singing the freshly written lyrics of "A Cowboy's Dream".

There was a guy there who called himself Flash Cadillac, and he spoke up when I'd finished. "Mel Tillis is doing a new album and he needs one more song to finish. If you want me to, I'll pitch this one for you."

Three days later, I recieved a call saying I needed to come to Nashville to sign contracts for publishing and recording rights for my first major cut. *I was definitely, finally on my way!*

"A Cowboy's Dream" was the second release from the album *After All This Time*. We soon received word that it was going to be a video on the newly formed CMT channel.

I was invited to the filming where I met my first playboy centerfold. Her name was Kimberly McArther, and she was truly a Cowboy's Dream.

For the first time, I got to watch one of my songs climb the Billboard charts. Once it was even Pick Hit of the Week. That, in itself, almost guaranteed a successful record. It was playing on the radio and on TV, and because of Kimberly McArther, the song poster from the video was hanging in every office, club and restaurant even close to Music Row. We were the talk of the town and living large.

For some reason, the song only climbed midway up the charts in the top 100 but it stayed in the charts for several weeks after that. Good luck trying to find any remnant of that song today. It's like it never existed—almost like someone intentionally buried it. I was sure this was going to be the first of many more charting records I would pen. This was only the beginning of my song writing career.

How Not to Make it in the Music Business

"A Cowboy's Dream" video poster.

Chapter Ten

My piano player worked days as an accountant in Nashville. One day, she told me that John Hobbs, owner of the Nashville Palace, had invited her to his Christmas party at the Palace. She asked me if I'd like to go. She thought I might make some important contacts there, so I tagged along.

Liz had got to know Mr. Hobbs' mother, so we were invited to sit at their personal table. Also at the table were several members of the Grand Ole Opry. I remember Johnny Russel, Porter Wagoner, and Jack Green. I know there were several others, but I can't remember them now. Everyone was sitting around talking when a lanky young man came out of the kitchen wearing one of those tall white chef's hats, and he was carrying a large pot of soup.

"Ladies and gentlemen," John Hobbs said, "There goes the next superstar of Country music!"

Everyone laughed, and Johnny Russel said, "How you figure that, Hobbs?"

"Because I just spent a whole lot of money on him," John said. It wasn't long until Randy Travis was the CMA's New Horizon Artist of the Year.

♪ ♪ ♪

I'll never forget singing on a live radio show in Kentucky called *Live At Libby's*. Libby's was a huge dinner club with live entertainment every Saturday night. I was all about original songs in those days, but because of the fact that they had a house band who backed a lot of different singers, they insisted that you perform cover songs. Tom T. Hall's son was the band leader.

I sang two songs that night. My last song was a Garth Brooks song called "Much Too Young to Feel this Damned Old". The response was great. I always felt good when the audience liked what I did and showed appreciation with enthusiastic applause.

As I left the stage, a man approached me with his hand extended. "I'm Libby," he said. "I wanted to tell you how much I enjoyed your singing.

"Well, thank you," I replied.

He said, "You know, that's the second time I've heard that last song performed here, and I think that's the best

I've ever heard it done. Ask me who sang it last time," he said.

I just gave him a puzzled look as he smiled and said, "Garth Brooks!"

Now, I'm not sure if he was serious or just yanking my chain, but he sure did make me feel good!

Another place where I spent a lot of time was Buddy Killen's Stockyards Lounge. I made friends with Curtis Green, who performed in the upstairs lounge. I never walked in that he didn't have me up singing my songs.

One night, I was filling in for Curtis when a delegation of several state representatives from different counties of Tennessee came in after a long day on Capitol Hill. I still remember how much they drank that night because they had just passed DUI legislation that day. I hope none of them drove home.

One of those men, Tommy Burnette, was a colorful character who represented my part of the state. After I played a set and was about to take a break, he came up with his hand outstretched, and he said, "Jim, I didn't know you did this! You're pretty good at it."

I told him it was all I had ever wanted — to make it in the music business. I told him how excited I was to be performing at the Stockyards because a person could be discovered that way.

"You come down to Legislative Plaza this week, have lunch with me, and we'll find someone who can help you. Bring your guitar," he said.

A few days later, I showed up and had lunch with all the politicians on Capitol Hill. Afterward, he invited a couple of the representatives from other counties to come in and listen as I played a few songs. "Fellows, how can we help him out?" Tommy asked when I finished.

The representative from Green County spoke up then. "Tommy, I don't think we can. You think we see politics? Just go down on Music Row and I'll show you some politics! They're way out of *our* league."

That pretty much put a damper on the gathering. My politician friend thanked me for coming down and said he would keep doing what he could and see what he could find out.

♪ ♪ ♪

One night Curtis, the regular Stockyards Singer, asked me if I could come over to his house to write a song. He was looking for a song for an album project, and said he had an idea but he wasn't a writer. He felt sure I could write a song using his idea.

I won't tell you here what the song I wrote that night was because you probably wouldn't believe me anyway, but it was the beginning of the end of my love affair with Nashville. I was writing songs constantly in those days, and I didn't see anything special in this one, so I more or less forgot about it. I'd written it for Curtis for an album project he was planning, and I knew he would do me right.

Time passed, and I was eating in a Nashville restaurant one day when I heard a familiar melody and a familiar lyric by a new country artist playing on the radio. I got up and went straight to the Earnest Tubb Record Shop and bought a copy of that record. The writers' credits listed two of the biggest, hottest song writers in Nashville.

I can't even start to tell you the emotions I experienced for the next few days. I finally made an appointment with a music business attorney about a lawsuit, but he didn't help my angry feelings. He said that a judge looking at two successful writers would think I was just a wannabe trying to get some money and I would lose if I claimed to have written the song. He said that the only person he had ever known to win such a suit was one of the Beatles.

As I left his office, I felt myself sinking deep into depression. The fact that the song was a monster hit didn't help things any. Every time I turned on the radio, there it was, and my depression would deepen.

Jim Bowman

From the time I was a kid, I'd known that all I ever wanted was to be a success in the music business. Now, when I was almost there, it was stolen from me. I was hurt, mad, and couldn't see a future in the business for me if everything I did was shot down or stolen. What was the use?

I walked into the bedroom, sat down in the corner, and put a .357 Magnum to my head. I had pressure on the trigger, when I heard a little voice say, *"Wouldn't it be better to be a live anything than a dead musician?"*

Now, that was radical to me. I'd never thought of any life where I was anything but a singer/songwriter. On top of that, I recognized that voice. I'd heard it that night many years ago when I walked the aisles of that little country church. I dropped the gun and just sobbed for a long, long time. I was done with Nashville. I was done with music.

By the way, the song in question went on to win two Grammy awards and launched the new artist to super stardom. I have been told that it probably would've made me a half-million dollars. I later asked Curtis how they'd gotten the song. The night I wrote it, Curtis had recorded it on a little reel-to-reel tape recorder. He said he recorded some other songs on the other side of the tape and that he'd given that tape to Buddy Killen, the President of Tree Publishing Company.

Chapter Eleven

I got back into church with my family after that fateful day that was my turning point. That's how I delt with my demons. I couldn't be a disc jockey anymore, because I couldn't stand to play other people's records. I'd always loved to bow hunt and I had to do something, so I opened an archery shop in my hometown.

I didn't pick up a guitar for over a year. Slowly, the calluses on my fingers that had been there since I was a kid disappeared.

One day, business was slow and I saw my old guitar sitting over in the corner, so I walked over and picked it up. It was out of tune and dusty, so I had to clean it off and tune it. Soon, by force of habit, I was writing a song. Bowhunting was all I was thinking about those days, so I wrote a song about bowhunting legend, Fred Bear.

I guess you could call it destiny, but one summer I found myself at the state archery tournament. The big tent there had a band and free beer. Many of my shop customers were there too, and they were all drinking. So, when the band took a break they started yelling for me to get up and sing a song. It was plain they were not going to stop, so I borrowed a guitar and walked up to the mic.

"Since we're all bowhunters, here's a little song I wrote about everyone's hero, Fred Bear." When I finished, I was shocked by the response. The crowd went wild and kept clapping until I did an encore and sang it again.

When I finished, it happened again. I realized I was on to something and decided right then and there to write and record a tape of hunting songs to market for hunters. That decision would eventually take me to stages and hunting camps all over the planet as The Camo Cowboy. After my *Relections From Hunting Camp* tape came out, I started getting requests to perform at various hunting events where I would sell my tapes.

One day, I was sitting in my shop when the phone rang. When I answered, the voice on the other end asked, "Is this Jim Bowman, singer of hunting songs?"

"Yes, it is," I said. "Who's this?"

"This is Ken Beck of Black Widow Custom Bows," he said. "I just listened to your tape and I noticed you mentioned God at least six times in your songs. I have a couple of questions for you. You don't have to answer unless you want to."

"Okay," I said, "shoot."

"First of all, are you a Christian?" he asked.

"Why, yes, I am," I answered. "That's actually a priority in my life these days."

"Second question," he said. "How would you like to be in my fall catalog?"

"Okay, let me think about it. ... Okay!" I said.

Ken Beck would end up becoming a very close friend.

I started getting booked quite a bit again, singing hunting songs for fellow hunters at outdoor events put on by organizations like Rocky Mountain Elk Foundation, Safari Club International, Pope and Young, and many others. Video Hunters and TV hunting shows began to want to use my songs in their projects. I became friends with many of the biggest celebrities in the hunting industry. Because of my hunting songs and returning to music, I found myself sitting in hunting camps around the world. I never dreamed this could happen. I was pretty content with life, but God was not through with me yet.

Chapter Twelve

Like a rerun, my phone rang again one day. This time, when I answered, the voice on the other end said, "You don't know me, but my name is Len Morris. I'm a movie producer, and I'm sitting here in the high desert of California with Roy Rogers, listening to a song he says you wrote for him."

I had. It was a tribute to my childhood hero, and I wanted him to hear it, so as my last act before I gave up on music, I'd put a tape in an envelope and mailed it to the Roy Rogers Museum in Victorville California.

"Just to be plain," I said, "you're talking about the king of the cowboys, right?"

He laughed. "Yes," he said. "We're doing an autobiographical movie about Roy' life, and he wants to use your song in the movie. What do you say?"

"Well, I say yes!" I practically screamed into the receiver. When I was a kid and being dragged from place to place, Roy Rogers had been the one constant in my life.

I lived in front of the TV on Saturday mornings, watching as ol' Roy saved the day.

No matter where we moved, I could always strap on my cap guns and find a kid willing to play *cowboys and outlaws* with me. Now, here I was a grown man and ol' Roy had my song, wanted to use it in a film and people were going to hear it!

I could never get anyone to tell me who would be singing the song. I figured it would probably be Clint Black or maybe Randy Travis, since they had both done projects with Roy.

Anyway, the movie was going to premiere on AMC and was called *King of the Cowboys*. My wife, Doris, planned a party at our home for the night of the premier. The invitations said, "Dress Western."

She invited many of our family and friends to whom she fed western barbecue. I was like a kid again, sitting on the edge of my chair as the movie began. I had goosebumps as I listened to the life story of Lenord Sly, known to the world as Roy Rogers.

A scene came on with Roy and Trigger in a children's hospital, and I heard myself begin to sing "What Ol Roy Would Do". He later told me that he didn't think anyone else could sing it with the passion he heard when I sang it. He said that every time he listened to it that he could see all the faces of the kids that lined up to see him at

The first time I met ol Roy. I was singing his song.

Madison Square Gardens, so he used the tape I had sent to him instead of getting someone else to sing it.

After the movie premier, I started getting calls — people wanted me to appear at western film festivals and memorabilia shows. I started writing cowboy songs and soon found myself back on the road as a singing cowboy.

The president of the Roy Rogers Fan Club, a fellow by the name of Jim Wilson, became a close friend and helped me get a lot of bookings. Somehow, I had known it would happen when I was just a boy. I would say, "When I grow up, I'm going to be a singing cowboy just like Roy Rogers!"

One show that I particularly remember was in Hollywood, and it was called the Western Fan Awards. As I performed there, practically every living old B western movie star I had ever watched was in the audience. They loved me, and they told me so. I don't know how many of them said, "Kid, if things were like they used to be, I'd get you into pictures!"

The only star absent that night was Roy. He was unable to come because of an obligation, but his son Dusty was on the show with me. When it was over, he came over and introduced himself and told us that his dad had invited us to come visit him at the museum before we went home. He said he'd like to put a face with the singer of the song.

The next day, Doris and I rented a car and drove up to Victorville. We got to the museum a few minutes before it opened, and the waiting area was full of people. When ol' Roy came in, he was in full "cowboy hero attire" with Dusty in tow. Dusty immediately brought him over and introduced us to him.

Roy turned around to all the people waiting and said, "I have a deal for you. If you don't mind waiting a little while longer to see the museum, you can get in free. I'd like to take my friends here for a little personal tour."

We entered the display area where all my childhood memories were on display. As I looked down the aisles, I could see saddles, guns, clothes, and hats that I'd pretended I was wearing a million times. I was anxious to see everything!

Roy took us over to a huge picture of the Rogers family. He proceeded to tell us everyone's name and something about each person in the picture. It was plain to see he loved his family and was very proud of them.

For the rest of the afternoon we looked at treasures he'd collected throughout his long movie and TV career. We saw Nellybelle the Jeep, Trigger Junior, and Bullet the Wonderdog. Trigger, who had been stuffed after his death, was displayed in a room protected by a large glass window. I know I must've looked like a kid with my nose pressed against the glass. Here was the horse I'd ridden a million miles in my imagination.

Roy got his keys out, opened the door and led me over to his great palomino. Then he reached down, grabbed my hand, and put it on Triggers neck. "I called him the old man," he said. "He wasn't just a horse. He was my movie partner and my friend. He could spin on a dime and give you change!"

When I looked at Roy, there were tears running down his cheek. When we got back to the waiting área, I was handed a guitar and I sang the song that I'd written for my childhood hero to my childhood hero. When I finished, he smiled and applauded. I had just given a King's Command Performance and the King liked it!

Chapter Thirteen

I guess the next few years were some of my favorite times because I was getting to live the Cowboy way. Everywhere I traveled I was "a hat act" — sharing the stage with other great western entertainers like Don Edwards, Waddie Mitchell, Red Stegal, Riders in the Sky and many others. I played at events for The Single Action Shooting Society like End of Trail and Shootout at Mule Camp. I even wrote the official SASS song for which I was presented a .44 Black Powder pistol customized with my SASS badge number and the SASS logo on the grips at End of Trail.

I met so many of the old B western movie stars and Saturday morning cowboys as I called them at the film festivals. A few I remember are Lash Larue, Gail Davis (TV's Annie Oakley) Buck Taylor, and William Smith.

Buck Taylor's dad was veteran actor, Dub Taylor. Dub was best known as a character actor and had been Red

Talking to Don Edwards.

Rider's side kick. In later years, he became a regular on *Hee Haw*.

Anyway, I traveled down to Georgia, where Dub was from, for a festival held to honor him and name him a favorite son of the Peach Tree state. After I got there, the promoters looked me up to ask me for a favor. "You're getting quite a reputation as a song writer," they said. "Do you think you could write a song about Dub and sing it when you perform?"

No pressure there! My answer was, "I'll try." So I spent the afternoon writing. That night, I performed the song

I wrote. Buck was sitting at the front table with his wife. I could see tears running down his cheek as I sang about his Dad.

When I finished my set, I walked over to his table and laid down the piece of paper I'd written the song on. "This is for you," I said and walked off.

A little bit later, he came over to the table where Doris and I were sitting. He bent over and extended his hand. "I ain't got the words, Pard," he said, "but thanks for this. I have a room in my house in Texas where I keep all of Dad's career stuff. I promise you that this will be framed and hung on the wall."

Another guy I met was William Smith. William had started off as a cowboy star and worked his way up to be a pretty well-known movie star. You might remember him as the bare-knuckle boxer who fought Clint Eastwood in the "Any Which Way" movies.

I first met him after I got into a rowdy debate with his woman in one of the courtesy rooms provided for the stars at the events. I was just sitting there listening to these ladies trashing two things that I dearly love — hunting and guns. I could tell they'd been brainwashed by their little Hollywood lefty groups. When I couldn't take it anymore, I entered the conversation, and we debated

Me with William Smith.

for probably 30 minutes. Finally, my pretty little opponent smiled and said, "Jim, I've never heard many of the points you just made. I guess I need to do more research."

Doris and I met them at several film festivals after that. They were always in the audience when it was time for me to sing. I really liked William Smith.

I was performing at a banquet in Hollywood one night and my wife and I found ourselves seated at a table

How Not to Make it in the Music Business

When I sang a song I had written called "Old Cowboys" Richard Farnsworth laughed and said, "It sounds just like me and Wilford Brimley!"

with Lyle Waggoner and his wife. If you remember the old *Carol Burnett Show*, he was always the good looking guy in every skit.

We were making small talk around the table and I was telling how Doris's great-great grandfather and grandmother had come across the mountains into Tennessee in a covered wagon. I mentioned that her grandmother was one half Cherokee Indian.

All at once Mrs. Waggoner came alive. "Oh she has Native American blood? Have you had her registered?" she asked.

I wasn't sure what she was talking about so I just sat there looking at her, so she went on, "You know there are all kinds of government grants you can get if you have her registered."

Doris was sitting there listening and she never said a word. All at once it struck me as funny, and while I was laughing I said, "Lady we're from the south where we register our horses and our coon dogs — *not* our wives!

Thank goodness about that time they introduced me from the stage and I had to go up and sing.

Chapter Fourteen

At a film festival in Charlotte, North Carolina, I had the privilege to meet James Best. He'd been a character actor for years in motion pictures when the role of TV Sherrif Rosco P. Coletrain, came along on *The Dukes of Hazzard*. They seat the celebrities at tables where the festival goers can meet them and get an autograph At the film festivals. I was lucky enough to be seated by Mr. Best and his lovely wife. We talked a lot during those two days, and I learned a lot about him.

For instance, I never knew he was an artist who painted with watercolors. I really liked him, so on Saturday afternoon I sneaked back to my hotel room, got out my guitar and wrote him a song. It was a funny little song about Rosco and the Dukes.

That night at the banquet I sang it to end my performance. James Best and his wife were seated right in front of me. Before I knew what was happening, he jumped up

Me and James Best aka Roscoe P. Coltrain.

on the stage, grabbed the mic, and in his Rosco P. Coletrain voice, yelled, "It's a good thing you did that, boy. I was about to have to cuff ya and stuff ya!"

The crowd went wild!

I've always been in awe of the power of a song. After I wrote "What Ol' Roy Would Do", I always closed my shows with it. I can't even start to tell you how many grown men and women I saw come to the stage with tears running down their faces to tell me that he'd been their hero, too.

I ran into Roy several times at shows after we saw him at the museum. I'm here to tell you, he was really a great man. After you were with him for five minutes, you forgot who he was because he was asking all about you. He was down to earth, for sure, but I've been at events where almost everyone in the room was a "somebody". When Roy and Dale entered the room, you could tell by the crowd that they were Hollywood royalty.

I played one year at the Cowboy Music and Poetry Symposium in Tuson, Arizona. It was held at a Holiday Inn there, and I was one of the scheduled singers. Doris and I were at the desk registering when someone walked up and said, "Excuse me, there's someone wanting to see you."

We were escorted to another part of the building and led into a private dining room. There were Roy, Dale, Dusty and several other members of their family sitting there eating. Dale spoke up and said, "Don't just stand there, sit down and join us!"

Roy had worked his way through his meal and had already had one bowl of ice cream when he saw another bowl sitting there. "Anybody going to eat this?" he asked. Nobody said a word, so he reached and grabbed it.

He looked over at me and asked, "Wonder what ol' Gene Autry's doing today?" Then the King of the Cowboys winked at me.

Later that night, at the University of Arizona, Roy Rogers, Dale Evans, Dusty, and the Sons of the Pioneers performed "Happy Trails" for the last time ever on stage. Because I was a featured artist at the festival, I was allowed to join them and sing along. *Wow!*

One of the saddest days I remember was the day ol' Roy passed away. We knew he was in the hospital but didn't realize how sick he'd been. Late in the morning that day I recieved a call from some folks in Portsmouth, Ohio, asking if I'd be willing to do something for them. Portsmouth was Roy's hometown and they wanted to have a memorial there at the same time the funeral was going on in California. So we did.

There is a 25-foot mural of Roy on a rearing Trigger there on the flood wall of the Ohio River. I gave a eulogy and sang "What Ol' Roy Would Do" standing in front of that mural. I'm glad I was able to give something back to the childhood hero who had given so much to me. Today, that still stands out as one of my most precious memories.

How Not to Make it in the Music Business

Roy Rogers Memorial in Roy's hometown of Portsmouth, Ohio.

Chapter Fifteen

A year later, I went back to California for End of Trail, a SASS cowboy shooting event. We decided to rent a car and drive back up to the museum for maybe the last time. The day Roy had given us that first museum tour I asked him this question, "Why don't you have any of your archery equipment on display? I remember seeing you on the *Ed Sullivan Show* trick shooting with a long bow. I also remember your picture on one of the comic books with a bow and arrows."

He got the funniest look on his face when he said, "Jim, in all the years I've had this museum, you're the first one to ever asked me that. I used to love bowhunting. I even hunted with Howard Hill and Earl Flynn!"

There'd been some changes at the museum since we'd last been there. In the hallway, they'd built a little island display, and it was full of ol' Roy's bows with quivers full of arrows. They'd also built a little theater where you could go in and watch Roy's movies.

It just so happened that they were showing the project that had my song in it that day. As we stood there looking at the archery equipment, I heard myself singing from the theater. I already had chill bumps when Doris said, "I think he's trying to tell you something."

Afterward, I drove up to his grave, sat down on a little bench there, and just talked to him for a bit. Before I left, I said, "Thanks, Roy. See you on down the trail."

Chapter Sixteen

I went into business with another musician friend in Cookeville, Tennessee. We opened a music store with a recording studio in the back. During that period I even had the opportunity to teach a songwriting class at Tennessee Tech.

One day, George, my partner, said, "Why don't you ride to Nashville with me today? I have an appointment to meet with Dean Dillon down at Opryland Records. I think you'd enjoy talking to him."

Now, I'd sworn off Nashville at this point. I hated it. It was almost like an ex-wife, holding nothing but bad memories for me. But, Dean Dillon is a legend in the music business. He wrote many of the big hits recorded by George Straight. So I reluctantly tagged along.

When we went into the Opryland building, I was surprised that the secretary knew my partner. "Hello, George," she said. "Dean stepped out for a few minutes, but you're welcome to go up and wait in his office."

When we got off the elevator by Dean's office, there was this scraggly looking kid standing there, wearing a University of Tennessee football jersey. He immediately struck up a conversation. "You guys songwriters?" he asked.

"He is," George said, pointing to me.

The kid said, "Hey, come on in here and play me something." By then, he was handing me his Takemine guitar. So, I played a couple of my songs for him and set down the guitar.

"Hey that's good stuff," he said. "I'd love to do some co-writing with you sometime. You up for it?"

"Sure," I said.

About that time, we saw Dean getting off the elevator and went on down to his office. On the way home, I said something about writing with the kid and George said, "Forget about that kid. He's from Knoxville. My dad plays golf with his dad. He's a banker. He's just down here to keep him off the streets and out of trouble.

The next time I saw Kenny Chesney, he was the Best New Country Artist of the Year. Every time I see George, he smiles and says, "Need anymore good career advice?"

I never did regain a desire to try Nashville again. I'd lost the fire. My priorities had changed. I still love to sing for people and I still write songs, but now I just write what I want to write instead of worrying about whether it's hit material.

I continued to play for a long time on a circuit that I'd built up over the years. The gigs I knew I could depend on started to dry up after Barack Obama was elected president. I don't know why, but many of the venues just quit holding events they'd hosted for years. Even the ones that continued cut their entertainment roster.

I haven't talked much about the spiritual part of my journey, but I think it's important right about here to do so. Show business is, by its very nature, a career that does not lend itself to such things because there is really no room for them. You get consumed with "me" and how can "I" succeed. You find yourself worshipping the idols of "self" and "stardom".

The Bible plainly tells us, "Thou shalt have no gods before Me." When you're in show business, career becomes your God.

I'm thankful I never got into drugs during my quest for fame. Throughout my career they were all around me, and I could've gone there anytime. Thank goodness I never did.

Alcohol was another matter. I probably consumed enough beer, whiskey, tequila, and rum to float my house.

The funny thing is, I never really drank for the enjoyment of it. I made my living entertaining folks who got drunk, and the only way I could survive and be around them was to be drunk first, so I usually was.

I tell my grandkids that everything I did in my life that I'm ashamed of and wish I could take back was done while I was drinking. Thank goodness, when I decided to quit, it had no hold on me. I just walked away and never looked back.

The definition of sin is anything that separates you from God. As I traveled the path I'd chosen, I found myself getting farther and farther from God. The road I was on was headed into darkness, away from "the Light of the world." We are talking here about a long road, one I was on for years.

Life is full of highs and lows, mountaintops and valleys, that's especially true for entertainers. I look back sometimes and ask myself, *Would you do it all over again?* My answer is usually no. There was too much pain and disappointment.

I remember vividly the place I was in when it all changed. I was empty. I was broken. I'd given it everything I had and come up empty. I was a spiritual train wreck, and my marriage was on the rocks. I asked myself a hard question: "Is this all there is?"

In that moment, I fell to my knees and surrendered my life to God. I remember literally holding my hands out and saying, "Here's my life. I've tried everything I know to make something of it and I can't. Lord, if you can use it, please take it!"

As soon as I said that, I instantly felt release and I know I became a different person.

Funny things started to happen after that. At the hunting shows, I started being asked to stay another day after my Saturday night performances so I could give my testimony in a Sunday morning worship service. Same thing happened at the cowboy shows. I was asked many times to help with cowboy church.

I found I had a great love for that. Soon, I was being asked to sing and speak at wildlife dinners and at Christian Hunting Camp events.

I remember the first time a pastor in Missouri turned his Sunday morning pulpit over to me, and I was allowed to solo as I brought the gospel message. Of all the things I did throughout my career, the most important were spiritual. There were people who came into God's kingdom not because of me, but because I happened to be there to tell them about the good news of Christ. Those things are of eternal significance.

I think my favorite story concerning this part of my life concerns one of the many friends I made through my hunting songs. Doris and I were sitting in our living room enjoying a quiet evening one night when the phone rang. When I answered, the voice on the other end said,

"You don't know me, Mr. Bowman, but I'm sitting on top of a mountain in Colorado in an elk camp. I'm talking to you on a satellite phone. Dr. David Roose just introduced me to your hunting music CD, and I'd like to order one so it will be waiting for me when I get home."

Now, David Roose is a Methodist minister from Michigan and a bowhunter supreme. He's also a friend and founder of Christian Bowhunters of America. I've sung in many gospel services for bow hunters where he presented the Word.

Before we hung up, I told my new friend, "Please tell Reverend Roose *thanks* for pushing my music right along with the gospel!"

Oh, and that was not to be the only order I ever filled from a hunting camp. One such call even came in from South Africa!

How Not to Make it in the Music Business

Cowboy Church at "Shootout at Mule Camp" a SASS event in Georgia.

Chapter Seventeen

The night at the Bluebird Café that I referred to at the beginning of this book could've turned out differently, but the music business had started to change. Dick Clark had come to town and suddenly old road warriors who had paid their dues were no longer welcome. Nashville was looking to market to a younger audience. "Old folks," they said, "love the music, but they don't buy records or tickets. Young people do."

Those guys I talked about at the Bluebird were from Lionel Richies' company. After they heard me sing, I really think they meant to give me a record deal, but when I showed up the next day for lunch in the daylight, they noticed a few well-earned lines around my eyes.

"Jim how old are you?" one of them asked.

Well, my momma raised me to tell the truth, so I told them. They looked at each other, and one of them said, "Oh man, we have strict instructions not to sign anyone over 30 years old."

On the way home that day, I remembered how many times the Music Row moguls had told me, "You're just a kid. Go home and pay some dues, then come back and see us."

I really think if I'd had all the tools available to the kids coming up today, things might've been different. We didn't have cell phones. If you wanted to contact someone when you were away from home, you had to find a pay phone and make sure you had change for the call.

We didn't have all the computer stuff the young artists are using today, either. If you wanted to cut a demo, you had to save up your money and pay someone with a studio to record you. The new crop of singers can use computer programs like Protools to put down a profesional-sounding track right in their own room on their own laptop!

Then there's iTunes, where you can take your music straight to the people. In the old days, the only way anyone ever heard your music was if the moguls put you out there and said you were worthy.

I put songs onto a site called Reverb Nation today, and I've never received anything but positive response from the folks listening. I wish I could've done that when I was 20 years old.

Now, you can also do your own promotions on Facebook and many other social media sites, telling people where you're playing and all about your new CD project. You can even give them a sample on YouTube.

We couldn't do any of that in the good ol' days. Truth be told, I have many more fans out there who know my music today than I did in the days when I was busting my chops in Nashville. That's all because of social media. It just came along too late for my music career.

I sometimes think of an incident that happened years into my career. I was playing at a fair and it just so happened a really good gospel group from my hometown was playing there, too. I went to their bus for some howdies and neck hugging, but when the mama matriarch saw me she started dressing me down. "Jimmy Bowman," she said, "God will never allow you to make it in Country music. You are as good a gospel singer as I have ever heard and that's what he meant for you to be!"

You can't imagine how many times over the years those words have haunted me as I drifted off to sleep…

Although I didn't accomplish everything Charles and Edith Bowman's son dreamed of as a child, I have had an amazing life. I was never allowed to grab the brass ring, but I was *so* close *so* many times.

I've opened shows in front of thousands of people, while sharing the stage and the spotlight with the giants of entertainment. My songs have been on radio, TV and in movies. Seriously, I've done almost everything I ever wanted to do without that Brass Ring. There's only one thing I can think of that leaves me unfulfilled.

That one thing concerns a Saturday Night and the stage of the Grand Ole Opry…

The "other love of my life." I have always had horses and this was "the one." His name was Taj. He was a registered Arabian and he never let me down!

The original "Camo Cowboy" performing for the prestigious Pope and Young Club.

How Not to Make it in the Music Business

Taken at the world famous Bluebird Café the night of the opening paragraph of this book..

Every singing cowboy has to have a sidekick. Mine was the prettiest of them all. Here I am with my wife Doris at the flood wall in Portsmouth.

Happy Trails!

CPSIA information can be obtained
at www.ICGtesting.com
Printed in the USA
LVHW01s0452100318
569358LV00001B/1/P